Shanghai Oriental Sports
Center in China
The Shanghai Oriental
Sports Center in China

Meinhard von Gerkan
Nikolaus Goetze

Shanghai Oriental Sports Center in China

The Shanghai Oriental Sports Center in China

gmp FOCUS

jovis

gmp · Architekten von Gerkan, Marg und Partner

Verortung

Location

31° 14' N, 121° 28' O

Shanghai liegt im Mündungsgebiet des Jangtsekiang und ist auf seiner Gesamtfläche von über 6300 km² durchzogen von Flüssen und Kanälen. Subtropisches Monsunklima bestimmt die Atmosphäre; der Untergrund ist so weich, dass Hochhäuser spezieller Pfeilerkonstruktionen bedürfen, um nicht einzusinken.

Shanghai, das sind Superlative: Der größte Hafen der Welt, eine der größten Städte weltweit mit rund 24 Millionen Einwohnern und noch immer einer der wichtigsten Industriestandorte Asiens.

Shanghai sits on the Yangtze River Delta, and its total area of 6,300 square kilometers is traversed by rivers and canals. The atmosphere is determined by a subtropical monsoon climate; the substrate is so soft that skyscrapers require special pile constructions to prevent them from sinking into the ground.

Shanghai means superlatives: the largest port in the world, one of the world's largest cities with around 23 million inhabitants, and still one of Asia's most important industrial locations.

Peking Beijing
China
Shanghai

Shanghai … „das Leben selbst"

Shanghai, das ist Westen im Osten. Schon im 19. Jahrhundert war der Handelsplatz Shanghai kosmopolitisch: Briten, Franzosen, Japaner und US-Amerikaner kamen hier zusammen. Während der Nazi-Diktatur fanden Tausende Juden aus Deutschland, Österreich und Osteuropa hier Zuflucht. Als in den 1990er-Jahren die Sonderwirtschaftszonen Pudong eingerichtet wurden, nahm die Stadt erneut einen atemberaubenden Aufschwung und bestätigte damit die Einschätzung Aldous Huxleys, der in den 1930er-Jahren behauptet hatte, Shanghai, das sei „das Leben selbst".

Shanghai in Zahlen

Fläche:
6340,5 km²
Bevölkerung:
24.150.000

Shanghai … "Life Itself"

Shanghai is the west in the east. By the nineteenth century, it was already a cosmopolitan trading center: the British, French, Japanese, and Americans came together here. During the Nazi dictatorship, thousands of Jews fled here from Germany, Austria and Eastern Europe. When the Pudong Special Economic Zones were established in the nineteen-nineties, the city once again experienced a breathtaking upswing, thereby confirming the view of Aldous Huxley, who asserted in the nineteen-thirties that Shanghai was "Life itself."

Shanghai in Figures

Area:
6,340.5 square kilometers
Population:
24,150,000

Agglomeration Shanghai
Shanghai agglomeration area

Sportstätten und Städtebau

Meinhard von Gerkan

Vom Beginn unserer beruflichen Tätigkeit an hat uns durch alle Jahre die Beschäftigung mit Sportbauten begleitet. Ein Anliegen war es uns immer, Sportstätten als Orte zu gestalten, die zwangloser Kommunikation Raum geben und die Grenzen zwischen aktiver Betätigung und passivem Zuschauen offen und fließend ausbilden. Wir verstehen sie nicht nur als genormte Behälter zur physischen Ertüchtigung oder für den Wettkampf, wenngleich es für internationale Wettkampfstätten natürlich klare Vorgaben gibt: Erst dadurch, dass in Moskau und Los Angeles, in Rom oder Melbourne unabhängig von allen spezifischen örtlichen Bedingungen durch künstliche Bauten weitgehend gleiche Voraussetzungen geschaffen werden, ist es möglich, einen australischen Schwimmer mit seinen europäischen Konkurrenten im Kampf um wenige tausendstel Sekunden zu vergleichen. Sportstätten bedürfen also notwendigerweise enger Reglements.

Doch das Wort „Sport" kommt ursprünglich aus dem mittellateinischen „disportare", das „sich zerstreuen, vergnügen" bedeutet. Daher sollten Sportstätten als Orte der Öffentlichkeit verstanden und als solche von der Bevölkerung angenommen werden. Um dies zu erreichen, ist es notwendig, sie so zu bauen, dass sie sich der Allgemeinheit öffnen, sie an Stellen aktiven städtischen Lebens zu platzieren und so zu gestalten, dass das sportliche Geschehen en passant erlebt werden kann, sich beiläufig und ungezwungen Berührungspunkte zwischen aktivem Tun und passivem Teilhaben ergeben. Sportstätten sind also immer sowohl funktional als auch städtebaulich in bewusste Kontexte zu setzen.

Hier liegen die Anforderungen an den Architekten, denn mit architektonischen Mitteln können solche Berührungspunkte geschaffen werden und zudem Anregungen zur Freizeitgestaltung, Möglichkeiten zum zwanglosen Verweilen.

Diesen Grundüberlegungen ist auch der Entwurf des Shanghai Oriental Sports Center (SOSC) verpflichtet. Geplant und gebaut anlässlich der FINA Schwimmweltmeisterschaften 2011, besteht der als Parkanlage konzipierte Komplex aus einem Schwimmstadion, einem Außenbecken, einem multifunktionalen Hallenstadion und einem Medienzentrum.

„Schaffe die Einheit in der Vielfalt. Erzeuge die Vielfalt in der Einheit", lautet eine unserer vier Maximen. Das SOSC ist ein gelungenes Beispiel dafür, wie man diese Maxime auf den verschiedensten Ebenen architektonisch umsetzen kann, denn auf Vielfalt sind wir bei diesem Projekt an zahlreichen Punkten gestoßen: mit den verschiedenen Bauten des Ensembles, den verschiedenen zu erfüllenden Funktionen und dem städtebaulichen Umfeld. Doch gerade, wenn man so vielfältigen Belangen gerecht werden will, besteht die Gefahr, dass ein Entwurf zerfasert. Unterschiede zu verbinden, ohne ihre Vielfalt zu minimieren – das war einer der wesentlichen Aspekte beim Entwurf der Anlage: Verbindendes Element zwischen den verschiedenen Sportstätten, aus denen sich das SOSC zusammenfügt, war das Wasser, die einzelnen Bauten sind durch das architektonische Leitmotiv von Wellen und Segeln charakterisiert. Zugleich bieten die offenen Wasserflächen die Möglichkeit, das Gelände in sein Umfeld einzubinden.

Funktionale Vielfalt bedeutet nicht nur, dass einzelne Bauten unterschiedlich genutzt werden, sondern eben auch die Verzahnung zwischen Geschlossen und Offen. Auf dieser Ebene ist das Ziel, das Viele in die Gemeinsamkeit zu binden, ein Gebot nicht nur der wirtschaftlichen, sondern vor allem der gesellschaftlichen und ökologischen Vernunft. Eine Schwimm- oder eine Fußballweltmeisterschaft darf der Anlass sein, ein Stadion zu bauen, aber nicht der einzige Grund. „Zwischen einer Sportveranstaltung und einem European Song Contest existieren nur noch wenige Unterschiede", schreibt Dirk Meyhöfer in seinem Essay. Das mag überspitzt sein, bringt aber die immer wichtiger und immer kompromissloser werdenden Bedingungen kommerzieller und medialer Mehrfachverwertbarkeit von öffentlichen Sport- und Veranstaltungsbauten auf den Punkt. Für die Stadt gibt es jedoch ein Leben nach der Großveranstaltung, und wenn die Architektur dauerhaft Teil dieses Lebens und keine geld- und ressourcenverschwendende Dekoration sein soll, dann muss sie entsprechend vielfältige Angebote machen. Insofern ist die gelungene Beziehung zwischen Einheit und Vielfalt eine der Bedingungen für nachhaltiges Entwerfen.

→ Fortsetzung Seite 14

Sport Facilities and Urban Development

Meinhard von Gerkan

Since the beginning of our professional activities, we have concerned ourselves over the years with sports buildings. It has always been important to us to design sports facilities as places that provide space for informal communication; we want them to be places where the boundaries between active performance and passive spectatorship are malleable. We do not see them only as standardized containers for physical exercise or competitions, although there are of course clear guidelines for international venues: it is only because largely identical conditions are created with artificial constructions in Moscow and Los Angeles, Rome, or Melbourne, independently of any specific local conditions, that it is possible to compare an Australian swimmer to his European rivals in the fight for a few thousandths of a second. Sports facilities therefore necessarily require tight regulations.

Yet the word "sport" originally comes from the medieval Latin "disportare", which means "to disport/amuse oneself". Therefore, sports venues should be understood as public places and accepted as such by the population. To achieve this, it is necessary to build them so that they open themselves to the public, to place them at sites of active urban life, and to design them so that the sporting event can be experienced *en passant*, and that points of contact occur incidentally and informally between active and passive participation. Sports facilities must therefore always be placed in conscious contexts In terms of both function and urban development.

These are the demands made of architects. It is architecture that creates these contact points, that gives leisure activities form, and that provides opportunities for unplanned lingering.

The design of the Shanghai Oriental Sports Center (SOSC) is also committed to these basic considerations. Designed and built for the FINA World Aquatics Championships in 2011, the complex conceived as a park consists of a swimming stadium, an outdoor pool, a multifunctional indoor stadium, and a media center.

"Create unity in diversity. Generate diversity in unity," is one of our four maxims. The SOSC is an excellent example of how to implement this maxim architecturally on various levels because we encountered diversity in this project at numerous points: with the various buildings of the ensemble, the various functions to be performed, and the urban environment. But particularly when you want to satisfy such diverse interests, there is a danger of the design becoming unraveled. One of the key aspects in the design of the complex was connecting differences without minimizing their diversity: the connecting element between the various sports venues that go to making up the SOSC is water, the individual buildings being characterized by the architectural leitmotif of waves and sails. At the same time, the open water areas offer the possibility to integrate the site into its environment.

Functional diversity means not only that individual buildings are used in different ways, but also that the closed and the open are interlinked. At this level, the goal of integrating the diverse into a commonality is a requirement that makes sense not only economically but, above all, socially and ecologically. A swimming or football world championship may occasion the building of a stadium, but it does not be the only reason for it. "Between a sports event and the European Song Contest there are only a few differences," Dirk Meyhöfer writes in his essay. That may be somewhat overstated, but it gets to the heart of the increasingly important and increasingly uncompromising conditions of the commercial and media-related multi-usability of public sports and event facilities. For the city, however, there is life after the big event, and if the architecture is to be a permanent part of this life, and not a money- and resource-squandering decoration, it must offer great diversity accordingly. In this respect, the successful relationship between unity and diversity is a condition for sustainable design.

→ Continued on page 14

Jenseits aller ästhetischen, funktionalen und kulturellen Verbindungen innerhalb des SOSC ist die Frage nach dem urbanen Kontext womöglich die wichtigste für den Entwurf gewesen. Das Gelände des SOSC war eine Industriebrache in unmittelbarer Nachbarschaft des Areals der Weltausstellung 2010, deren Motto passenderweise lautete: „Better City - Better Life". Ohne eine nachhaltige Stadtentwicklung bleibt das nicht mehr als ein schöner Spruch. Das SOSC ist deswegen eine Sportanlage, aber auch eine Park- und Erholungsanlage. Architektur muss auf Kontexte reagieren, und sie muss auch Kontexte schaffen. Die Verbindungen, die das SOSC zu seinem städtebaulichen Umfeld aufbaut - die Art und Weise, wie es sich darin einfügt, es vervollständigt und erweitert -, mögen nicht ganz so offenkundig sein wie die architekturästhetischen Bezüge innerhalb des Ensembles selbst. Aber es sind nicht zuletzt diese Verbindungen, die das SOSC zu einem wichtigen Bestandteil der auf Integration setzenden städtebaulichen Entwicklung Shanghais - und damit zu einem der Vorzeigeprojekte unseres Büros machen.

Besides all the aesthetic, functional, and cultural connections within the SOSC, the question of urban context was perhaps the most important one for the design. The site of the SOSC was an industrial wasteland in the immediate vicinity of the site of the World Expo 2010, the motto of which was, fittingly: "Better City–Better Life." Without sustainable urban development, that is nothing more than a catchy phrase. The SOSC is therefore a sports complex, but also a park and recreation facility. Architecture must respond to contexts, and it must also create contexts. The connections that the SOSC establishes with its urban environment–the way it fits into it, complements it, and extends it–may not be quite as obvious as the architectural and aesthetic references within the ensemble itself. But it is not least these connections which make the SOSC an important element of the integration-oriented urban development of Shanghai–and one of the flagship projects of our office.

Ensemble am Wasser – das Shanghai Oriental Sports Center

Nikolaus Goetze

Shanghai, am Fluss Huangpu nahe der Jangtsekiang-Mündung gelegen, ist von Wasserwegen durchzogen, und so sind sowohl die Wirtschaftskraft der Stadt als auch ihre urbanen und landschaftlichen Qualitäten eng mit dem Element Wasser verknüpft. Während sich die chinesische Altstadt, die kolonialzeitlichen und neueren Stadtstrukturen westlich des Huangpu erstrecken, wurde seit den 1990er-Jahren der Stadtteil Pudong östlich des Flusses entwickelt. Die historisch bereits wirtschaftsstarke Stadt Shanghai und die neuen Sonderwirtschaftszonen in Pudong bilden über den Huangpu hinweg den „Drachenkopf" der chinesischen Wirtschaft. Am Huangpu-Ufer in Pudong liegt, eingerahmt von einem weiteren Wasserlauf, nahe dem Areal der EXPO 2010 das Grundstück des Shanghai Oriental Sports Center (SOSC), Austragungsort der FINA Schwimmweltmeisterschaften 2011, für das 2008 ein Wettbewerb ausgelobt wurde. In Sichtweite überspannen mehrere Bogenbrücken die angrenzenden Wasserwege. Folglich wurden Wasser und Brücken als verbindende und für die Region charakteristische Elemente als Entwurfsthema im Wettbewerb aufgegriffen.

Drei Stadienbauten – Mehrzweck- bzw. Hallenstadion, Schwimmstadion bzw. Natatorium und Außenschwimmstadion – sowie ein Hochhaus als Medienzentrum sind um Wasser- und Grünflächen arrangiert, die die Gebäude als öffentliche Bereiche verbinden. Der zentrale See hat nach Norden eine weiche Uferlinie, die der runden Form des erhöht gestellten Mehrzweckstadions folgt, während er im Süden durch das rechtwinklige Schwimmstadion eine harte Kante erhält. Eine Landschaftsbrücke verbindet das Areal über eine trennende Schnellstraße hinweg zum mondsichelförmigen Außenschwimmstadion, das sich in ebenfalls erhöhter Lage zum Huangpu hin öffnet.

Eine extrem kurze Planungs- und Bauzeit von lediglich zweieinhalb Jahren führte zur Entscheidung, zur Vermeidung unübersichtlicher Genehmigungsprozesse keine sichtbaren Konstruktionen zu planen. In den solitären Großformen sind die Strukturelemente selbst sichtbar, die Konstruktionselemente jedoch verkleidet. Das konstruktive Motiv der parallel gereihten weißen Bögen erinnert an Segel in vollem Wind, während die Überbrückung der großen Spannweiten klar in den Elementen ablesbar bleibt und damit eine Analogie zu den nahen Brückenbauten bildet.

Den sehr unterschiedlichen Anforderungen an Funktion und Größe folgend, hat jedes der Stadien seine eigene markante Form. Die einheitliche Formensprache der Strukturelemente und Fassaden aber vereint die Solitäre zu einer Gebäudefamilie.

Die Stahlkonstruktionen der Rahmen, Bögen bzw. Kragarme sind mit doppelt gekrümmten, weiß beschichteten Aluminiumpaneelen verkleidet, deren konkave Oberflächen jeweils perfekte Kugelausschnitte bilden.

→ Fortsetzung Seite 20

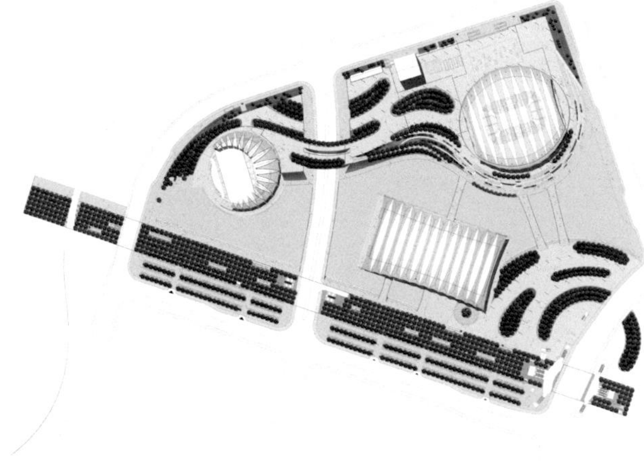

Lageplan
Site plan

Ensemble on the Water–the Shanghai Oriental Sports Center

Nikolaus Goetze

Shanghai, located on the Huangpu River near the Yangtze estuary, is traversed by waterways, and so both the economic might of the city and its urban and scenic qualities are closely linked to the element of water. Whereas the Chinese Old City, the colonial-era and more recent city structures extend west of the Huangpu, since the nineteen-nineties the Pudong District has been developed to the east of the river. The historically economically strong city of Shanghai and the new special economic zones in Pudong form the so-called dragon's head of the Chinese economy across the Huangpu.

On the banks of the Huangpu in Pudong, framed by a further watercourse and near the EXPO 2010 site lies the Shanghai Oriental Sports Center (SOSC), the venue of the 2011 FINA World Aquatics Championships, for which an architectural competition was initiated in 2008. Several arched bridges span the adjoining waterways within view. Consequently, water and bridges were taken up as connecting and regionally characteristic elements in the design theme for the competition.

Three stadium structures–a multi-purpose stadium, an indoor stadium called Natatorium and an outdoor swimming stadium–and a high-rise building as a media center are arranged around water and green areas that link the buildings as public zones. The central lake has a soft shoreline to the north, which follows the round form of the elevated multi-purpose stadium, whereas it has a hard edge in the south due to the rectangular swimming stadium. A landscape bridge over a separating highway links the area to the crescent-shaped outdoor swimming stadium that opens onto the Huangpu River from its similarly elevated location.

An extremely short planning and construction period of only two and a half years led to the decision not to plan any visible constructions in order to avoid complicated approval procedures. The structural elements themselves are visible in the large, individual shapes of the buildings, but the construction elements are cladded. The constructional motif of the parallel white arches evokes sails full of wind, while the bridging of the wide spans remains clearly visible in the elements, thereby creating an analogy to the nearby bridge constructions.

In keeping with the highly differing requirements regarding function and size, each of the stadia has its own distinctive shape. However, the uniform design idiom of the structural elements and façades unites the solitary components to form a family of buildings.

The steel constructions of the frames, arches, and cantilevers are cladded with double-curved, white-coated aluminum panels whose concave surfaces each form perfect spherical sectors.

For the round-floored, multi-purpose stadium, ten frame trusses are arranged in parallel, forming the façade and roof construction. On both sides and parallel to the middle pair of trusses with a span of 170 meters there are four axisymmetrical truss pairs, which encompass an all-encircling, thirty-five-meter-high glazed foyer.

The elongated Natatorium containing four adjacent pools consists of in-line, arch-shaped triangular trusses along which glazed skylights permit filtered daylight to enter.

→ Continued on page 20

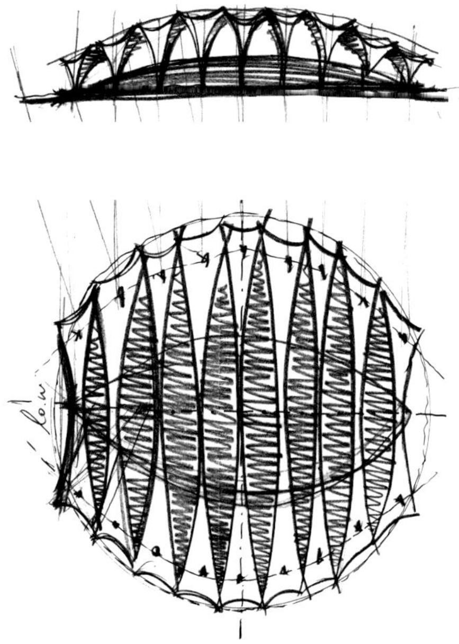

Skizze
Sketch

Visualisierungen von Mehrzweckstadion, Außenschwimm-stadion, Medienzentrum und Natatorium
Visualization of multi-purpose stadium, outdoor swimming stadium, media center and Natatorium

Für das im Grundriss runde Mehrzweckstadion sind zehn Rahmenbinder parallel arrangiert, die die Fassaden- und Dachkonstruktion ausbilden. Beidseitig und parallel zum mittleren Binderpaar mit einer Spannweite von 170 m sind achsensymmetrisch vier jeweils kürzere Binderpaare gestellt, die ein ringsum laufendes 35 m hohes verglastes Foyer umschließen.

Die langgezogene Schwimmhalle mit vier aneinandergereihten Beckenanlagen besteht aus gereihten, bogenförmigen Dreigurtbindern, entlang derer Streifen verglaster Oberlichter gefiltertes Tageslicht einfallen lassen.

Im Außenschwimmstadion mit Sprungturmanlage wird die halbrunde Tribünenüberdachung durch radial angeordnete Kragarme mit dazwischen gespannten leichten Membranen gebildet.

Die Fassade des 80 m hohen, im Grundriss quadratischen Medienzentrums nimmt die Materialität der Verkleidung der Stadienträger auf: Die Glasfassade des Gebäudes ist umschlossen von einer Hülle aus weißen, perforierten Aluminiumpaneelen, deren Lochungsmuster ein Wellenmotiv zeigt und damit einen Bezug zum Wasser herstellt.

Die Nachnutzung des Ensembles war ein wesentlicher Aspekt in der Planung der Gebäude wie auch der Gesamtanlage. Außenschwimmstadion und Schwimmhalle sind heute öffentliche Schwimmbäder. Das Mehrzweckstadion war zur Weltmeisterschaft temporär mit einem Edelstahlbecken ausgestattet, beherbergt in der Nachnutzung aber Sport- und Konzertveranstaltungen aller Art. Mobile Ränge erlauben eine Aufstockung von 14.000 auf 18.000 Zuschauerplätzen. Mit dieser groß angelegten Sportstätte kann sich die Stadt Shanghai auch in Zukunft um die Austragung internationaler Wettkämpfe bewerben.

Auf einer ehemaligen Industriebrache, ähnlich wie das Areal der Weltausstellung EXPO 2010 nach dem Motto „Better City, Better Life" entwickelt, entsteht im Umfeld des SOSC ein neuer Stadtteil mit Wohnvierteln, Einkaufsmöglichkeiten und Bürokomplexen. Das Gelände des SOSC wird für die Öffentlichkeit zugänglich sein und im Herzen der neuen Stadtentwicklung mit den schattigen Arkaden der Stadien, den großzügigen Wasserflächen und Grünanlagen wertvolle Freizeitflächen bieten.

In the outdoor swimming stadium with its diving platform, the semi-circular arena roof consists of radially arranged cantilevers with lightweight membranes spanned between them.

The façade of the eighty-meter-high media center with its square floor-plan takes up the materiality of the stadium's girder cladding: the glass façade of the building is enclosed in a shell of white, perforated aluminum panels whose hole pattern depicts a wave motif in a further allusion to water.

The subsequent use of the ensemble was a major aspect in the planning of both the buildings and the complex as a whole. the outdoor and indoor swimming stadia are now public swimming baths. The multi-purpose stadium was fitted temporarily with a stainless steel basin for the world championships but is now used for sports events and concerts of all kinds. Mobile tiers allow spectator seating to be increased from 14,000 to 18,000. With this generously designed sports venue, the city of Shanghai can also compete for the hosting of international events in the future.

Developed on former brownfield land—like the site of the EXPO 2010 World Exposition—under the motto "Better City, Better Life," a new district with residential areas, shopping facilities and office complexes is being created around the SOSC. The site of the SOSC will be accessible to the public. Right at the heart of the new urban development, the SOSC will offer valuable recreation areas with shady stadium arcades, spacious water areas, and green spaces.

Vogelperspektive
Bird's eye view

Perspektivenwechsel

Das Shanghai Oriental Sports Center liegt in China – wahrgenommen wird es aus der ganzen Welt

Ein Essay von Dirk Meyhöfer

Zu weit weg?

› Architekturwahrnehmung und Architekturkritik haben sich verändert, werden zusehends Opfer einer durch Digitalisierung forcierten Vermischung von Realität und Virtualität. Globaler sind sie geworden, manchmal regelrechte Ferndiagnosen, was häufig Voraburteile provoziert; assimiliert an internationale Bildwelten des Internets, verunsichert oder überformt durch Blogs und soziale Netzwerke; manchmal sogar nur Reflexion eines einzigen frühen Renderings. Architekturvermittlung ist heute mittelbar sowie medial und gehört den schnellen, den elektronischen Medien. Fast immer stehen die Objekte der Kritikerbegierde sehr weit weg. Das betrifft die Distanz, ausgedrückt in Meilen, es betrifft aber auch Kulturgrenzen, die es zu überwinden gilt. Eine besondere Spezies betroffener Projekte sind Sportbauten. Nicht die Dreifachturnhalle auf dem Gesamtschulcampus der eigenen Kinder, sondern eben die Anlaufstellen des interkontinentalen Sportbetriebes für FIFA, Olympia und andere World-Championship-Betriebe. Die gmp-Architekten gehören seit Jahrzehnten zu den Glücklichen, die in Technik, Konstruktion und Ausdruck die Arenen für die Sportarten der modernen Zeit geprägt haben. Das hat berechtigte Gründe, die zum einen in ungewöhnlich gelungenen Projekten liegen wie der grandiosen Wiedergeburt des Berliner Olympiastadions[1] (2006). Die Neuinszenierung des stigmatisierten Olympiastadions von 1936[2] wirkte bis weit hinein in das „Reich der Mitte" und gilt dort als ein Meisterwerk aus Verbindung von Geschichte und zeitgenössischer Konstruktion, die das Stadion für Chinesen zu einem Gesamtkunstwerk werden lässt. Zum anderen gehört zu solchen Großbauten auch eine gewisse Größenordnung des jeweiligen Büros, um auf hohem Niveau und unter großem Zeitdruck beispielsweise WM-Stadien für Südafrika oder Brasilien bauen zu können. Die Architekten von Gerkan, Marg und Partner erfüllen diese Kriterien.

1

Bei Sportbauten kommt das Wörtchen „groß" häufig vor. Und darin liegt manchmal in der Außenwahrnehmung ein Problem. Es hat sich eine Liga der internationalen Großbüros herausgebildet. Größe und Gigantismus, ja Selbstdarstellung sind inhärente Themen der medialen Diskussion, und häufig werden sie unreflektiert und ohne Ansehung des Einzelfalls negativ empfunden. So entstehen Klischees. Auch gmp sieht sich gelegentlich mit solcher Kritik konfrontiert. Dabei steht das Architektonische und Konstruktive nicht mehr im Fokus der Beobachtung. Hinzu kommt die Frage, ob sich denn nun die internationale Baukunst ausgerechnet mit „weißen Elefanten" schmücken sollte. Darunter verstehen Feuilletonisten gern riesige Bauwerke, die die meiste Zeit ihres Daseins nutzlos herumstehen, weil sie gar nicht mehr gebraucht werden bzw. ihre Bespielung nicht bezahlbar ist, wie beispielsweise im Fall des Olympiaparks in Athen.[3]› All das erschwert gelegentlich einen klaren und hoffentlich relevanten Blick auf solche Sportbauten.

Bekannt wurde ich mit dem Shanghai Oriental Sports Center (SOSC) schon im Herbst 2009, glücklicherweise in privilegierter Nahsicht, als ich mit der gmp-Projektleiterin und ihrem Team im Staub der Baustellenwege stand und riesige „Elefantenfüße" aus Stahl angeliefert wurden. Und das Planungsteam, bestehend aus Architekten von gmp und den beteiligten Partnerbüros, in einer Mischung aus Verzweiflung und laissez faire notierte, dass ihre Zeichnungen von den chinesischen Projektentwicklern mit großer Fantasie umgesetzt wurden. Für die neuen Sportstätten hatte erst ein Jahr zuvor, also genau zweieinhalb Jahre vor den eigentlichen Weltmeisterschaften im August 2011, ein Wettbewerb stattgefunden. Selbst für China ist das eine sehr sportliche Planungs- und Bauzeit.

Im Sommer 2011 sah ich dann das aufgrund seiner Größe eindrucksvolle Sportensemble wieder – mit den verbauten und verkleideten Stahlträgern. Das heißt, ich sah diese eben nicht, sondern wie Millionen anderer Zuschauer im öffentlich-rechtlichen deutschen

Changing Perspectives
The Shanghai Oriental Sports Center Is Located in China, and Perceived from All over the World

An essay by Dirk Meyhöfer

Too far away?

› Increasingly falling victim to the amalgamation of reality and virtuality as a a consequence of digitization, architectural perception and criticism have changed. They have become much more global, to the point of becoming telediagnoses, which provoke rash judgments. Architectural perception and criticism have become assimilated to the internet's international imagery, while being destabilized or re-shaped by blogs and social networks. Sometimes these images are no more than a reflection of a single, early rendering. Today, mediation of architecture is primarily media-related; and it is owned by the fast, the electronic media. The objects of critical desire are almost always very far away. This applies to the distance, expressed in miles, as well as to cultural boundaries that need to be overcome. A particular species of affected projects is sports facilities. Not the triple gymnasium on one's children's high school campus, but the meeting places of intercontinental sports for FIFA, the IOC, and other world championship organizers. For decades, gmp architects have been among the fortunate ones to have shaped arenas for the sports of the modern era in terms of technology, construction, and expression. There are legitimate reasons for this which lie, on the one hand, in exceptionally successful projects such as the grand rebirth of the Olympiastadion[1] in Berlin (2006). The revival of the stigmatized Olympiastadion from 1936[2] was appreciated as far away as China, where it was regarded as a masterpiece of combined history and contemporary design, which for Chinese standards makes the stadium a complete work of art. On the other hand, buildings of such a large scale also require a practice of a certain size in order to be able to build, for example, World Cup stadia for South Africa or Brazil to high standards and under great time pressure. gmp architects fulfill these criteria.

In the context of sports buildings, a little word that often crops up is "large." And herein, at times, lies a problem with regard to external perception. A league of international large practices has evolved. Size, gigantism, and, for that matter, self-presentation are inherent topics in media debate, and they are frequently perceived as being negative, without reflection and without consideration of the individual case in question. This is how stereotypes are born. gmp also occasionally sees itself confronted with criticism of this kind. Observations in this vein are no longer focused on architecture and construction. Compounding this problem is the question as to whether international architecture should be adorned with, of all things, white elephants. By this, columnists usually mean huge edifices which spend most of their existence standing around uselessly because they are no longer needed or because using them is too expensive, as in, for example, the Olympic park in Athens.[3] All of these complications at times make it difficult to consider such sports buildings in a clear and relevant light.

I had already made my acquaintance with the Shanghai Oriental Sports Center (SOSC) in autumn 2009 when I stood in the dust of the construction site with the gmp project manager and her team as giant "elephant's feet" made of steel were being delivered. And the planning team, consisting of architects from gmp and the participating partner practices, noted with a mixture of despair and laissez faire that their drawings had been implemented with a great deal of imagination by the Chinese project developers. A competition for the new sports venues had taken place only a year earlier, that is, exactly two and a half years prior to the actual World Championships in August 2011. Even by Chinese standards, that is a very "sportsmanlike" planning and construction period.

2

Fernsehen ganz andere Bilder, jene der gigantischen 14. FINA Schwimmweltmeisterschaften in Shanghai. Der Bildschirm war in schönes esoterisches Dunkelblau getaucht und grafisch geschmückt mit bunten Nationalwimpeln der teilnehmenden Nationen, mit Einblendungen von Sieger- und Verlierernamen, Zehntel- und Hundertstelsekunden. Architekturbilder? Vielleicht als Pausenfüller. Im Prinzip funktionieren solche Bauten heute wie Fernsehstudios, deren Flächen multifunktional zu nutzen sind. Zwischen einer Sportveranstaltung und dem European Song Contest existieren nur noch wenige Unterschiede, die im Wesentlichen die Szenografen bildnerisch bestimmen. Wir Deutschen hatten sowieso ganz andere Probleme, denn damals begann der bis heute andauernde lange Marsch weg von der Leistungsspitze im Weltschwimmsport.

3

Groß und trotzdem elegant?

› September 2011: Es ist ein großer Vorteil, wenn man mit einer Führung durch die Architekten in ein Objekt hinein darf. Auch wenn dann immer noch die Begegnung mit dem Bau kurz, ja so kurz ist, dass man die Phase des Fremdelns nicht überspringt, kommt man ihm doch näher. Und wenn man eben nicht die Sportstätten im Betrieb genießt. So bleiben dann Wahrnehmungen übrig, wie die westliche Besuchertruppe stark schwitzend versuchen muss, konzentriert Notizen zu machen, weil die großartige, notwendige, wunderbare Klimatisierung nach den Spielen abgeschaltet bleibt. Große Schwimmhallen und Mehrzweckarenen müssen auf Klima, das heißt auf die Lüftung für die hohen äußeren und inneren Belastungen ausgelegt werden, vor allem im subtropischen Shanghai. Und sie müssen ein Höchstmaß an Anforderungen an Licht- oder Beschallungstechnik für TV-Übertragungsqualitäten erfüllen. Zumindest das konnte das Fernsehbild positiv belegen.

Das SOSC ist trotzdem ein Vorzeigeprojekt deutscher Architektur und Ingenieurskunst geworden – aber auch der Freiraum- und Landschaftsplanung und des Städtebaus. Was für mich persönlich die wichtigste Leistung der beteiligten Planer und Ingenieure darstellt. Denn China hat Nachholbedarf, wenn es im unkontrollierten Wildwuchs mehr als nur das übliche Plankton der Megastadt produzieren will. Entstanden sind hier nicht nur Stadien, sondern ein für den gewöhnlichen chinesischen Städtebau richtungsweisender Landschaftspark mit drei großen Sportstätten und einem Presse- und Verwaltungszentrum – drei Mega-Kiesel am Wasser vor der gigantischen Kulisse Shanghais als Biotop für Menschen, nicht für Autos. Chinesische Architekten würden keine gemeinsame Linie für drei solche Bauwerke suchen, sondern Unikate. Die gmp-Architekten setzten auf Einheit und Harmonie im Ensemble. Mit einem Natatorium, einer multifunktionalen Großveranstaltungshalle und einem Freiluftschwimmstadion. Keine konkurrierenden selbstgefälligen Eigenbrötler, sondern Teamspieler in formaler Verwandtschaft mit durchgängigem Konstruktionsprinzip, aber mit angemessenen Variationen in der Anmutung. Im Gesamtergebnis ist dieser europäische Architekturkulturexport mit Präsens und Ludens durchaus vergleichbar mit jenem Ensemble aufgefalteter Tragwerke, das 1972 im Münchner Olympiapark[4] realisiert wurde. Man darf die Gebäude als kraftvolle, robuste Enkel der Gestalten von Günter Behnisch und Frei Otto betrachten, doch gelegen nicht im Bayrischen, sondern am Huangpu-Fluss, der Lebensader zwischen Alt-Shanghai und dem jungen, dynamischen Pudong.

Darf man? Trotz Kultur-Crossover, was zusätzlich gesellschaftskritische Unschärfe programmiert? Wenn nicht der damalige Anspruch gewesen wäre, die spielerischen

In the summer of 2011, I saw the sports ensemble again—impressive due to its size—with the installed and cladded steel girders. In fact, I did not see them in person, but—like millions of other viewers watching public German television, I saw completely different pictures, namely those of the gigantic 14th FINA World Aquatics Championships in Shanghai. The screen was immersed in a beautiful esoteric dark blue and graphically decorated with colorful national pennants of the participating countries, with overlays of winners' and losers' names, and tenths and hundredths of a second. Architectural images? Perhaps as intermission fillers. Basically, such buildings now function like television studios with multifunctional surfaces. Between a sports event and the European Song Contest there are only a few differences that are determined creatively to a large extent by the scenographers. Besides, we Germans had other problems entirely as this was when the long, still ongoing descent from the top echelons of world swimming began.

Big yet still elegant?

› September 2011: It is a major advantage to be allowed inside the building with the architects as tour guides. Even though the encounter with the building is brief—so brief, in fact, that one is still left with a sense of alienation afterwards—one feels closer to it. And especially if one has the chance to enjoy the sports venue outside business hours, other perceptions remain, such as the group of western visitors who must try to concentrate on their note-taking while sweating profusely because the splendid, necessary, wonderful air-conditioning stays switched off after the competitions. Large swimming stadia and multi-purpose arenas must be designed for climate, that is, for the ventilation of the higher external and internal loads, particularly in subtropical Shanghai. And they must meet extremely high demands with regard to light and sound technology for TV broadcasting qualities. At least that aspect was demonstrated well by the television pictures.

Nevertheless, the SOSC has become a showcase project for German architecture and engineering. Also for open space and landscape planning, as well as urban construction. To me personally, this is the most important achievement of the participating planners and engineers. Because China has some catching up to do if it wants to produce more than the usual megacity plankton of uncontrolled growth. What has been created here is not just stadia, but a landscape park that is pioneering by normal Chinese urban planning standards: with three large sports venues and a press and administration center—three mega-pebbles by the water in front of the gigantic backdrop of Shanghai as a biotope for people, not for cars. For three buildings like this, Chinese architects would not seek something common but rather something unique. gmp architects focus on unity and harmony in an ensemble: with indoor and outdoor swimming stadia and a multi-purpose large event hall. Not competing, complacent mavericks, these buildings function as team players

4

in a formal relationship with a consistent construction principle, yet with tailored variations in their look and feel. In the overall result, this European architectural cultural project with its presence and playfulness is comparable to the ensemble of unfolded support structures realized at Munich's Olympiapark[4] in 1972. We may regard the buildings as the vigorous, robust grandchildren of the figures created by Günter Behnisch and Frei Otto, not located in Bavaria, but on the Huangpu River, the lifeline between old Shanghai and the young, dynamic Pudong.

May we? In spite of the cultural crossover, which also inevitably leads to socio-critical fuzziness? If only it had not been the intention at the time for the playful architecture of the Munich Olympiapark to be ambassadors of a new, cheerful German spirit (which was then ousted and made impossible by terrorist attacks). And this cheerful spirit now applies in China? This raises the question: whose spirit does the SOSC stand for?

Architekturen des Münchner Olympiaparks als Botschafter eines neuen fröhlichen deutschen Geistes zu sehen (der dann von den Anschlägen verdrängt und unmöglich gemacht wurde). Und dieser fröhliche Geist gilt heute in China? Bliebe die Frage, für wessen Geist steht das SOSC?

Es geht bei guter Architektur nicht um Bilder und Allegorien, Vergleiche und Symbole allein, sondern um architektonische, um Stadt- und Landschaftsräume. Um die letzteren handelt es sich vor allem beim SOSC, weil die Innenräume vor allem ihren jeweiligen Funktionen gehören bzw. flexibel bespielbar wie ein Filmstudio zu sein haben, also austauschbar sind.

Draußen folgt die Komposition der Freiräume zunächst einem chinesischen Ansatz, wenn man so will. Denn die drei Stadionbauten sind an künstlich angelegten Wassern aufgezäumt; es wird sozusagen ein Makro-Feng-Shui-Gefühl aufgebaut und erzielt. Die Eingänge des Sportcampus wurden zum Süden hin orientiert. (Der Feind kam in China immer aus dem Norden, ebenso der kalte Wind aus der Mongolei.) Das uralte chinesische Thema, also das Motiv einer naturreligiösen Wasser-Park-Landschaft, nimmt von dort seinen Lauf. gmp überlagert jetzt diesen „grün-blauen" Sportcampus mit drei Hallenkomplexen: Den Auftakt bildet das sogenannte Natatorium mit mehreren tagesbelichteten Schwimmbecken auf 220 m Länge. Es liegt privilegiert am Hauptplatz mit der U-Bahn-Station. Das ist logisch so, denn in der Nachnutzung ist es ein öffentliches Schwimmbad geworden. Während der Weltmeisterschaften wurden die Becken vorwiegend zum Training genutzt. Das Natatorium ist ein Grenzgänger zwischen Campus und Stadt. Die äußere Kante der Schwimmhalle wirkt aber nicht wie eine starre Grenze: Die Dachträger, die durch zweifach gebogene Alupaneele verkleidet sind und in die Fassade überlaufen, werden durch dreieckige Glasflächen unterbrochen. Durch dieses Öffnen und Schließen der Fassaden entsteht der Eindruck von Arkaden. Durch den sich wiederholenden Rhythmus zwischen Träger und Öffnung wirken diese Arkaden auch bei dieser Länge leicht und locker.

Es folgt dann im „Hinterland" eine Multifunktionsarena, die während der FINA Weltmeisterschaften als Hauptwettkampfstätte der Schwimmdisziplinen genutzt wurde. Sie fasst 18.000 Zuschauer. Bei meinem damaligen Besuch wurde gerade die Beeisungstechnik unter den Hallenboden eingebaut. Die Arena ist nun ein Hybrid für Sport-, Konzert- und andere Kulturveranstaltungen. Geschwommen wird hier nicht mehr, dafür ist sie auch kein weißer Elefant geworden. Die auf einem sechs Meter hohen Stahlbetonpodium positionierte Halle mit 130 bis 140 m Durchmesser und lichter Höhe (45 m) besitzt auf fast runder Grundrissfläche eine Hauptkonstruktion für Fassade und Dach aus parallelen Dreigurtbindern. Ich schrieb damals in einer Kritik mit dem Schwerpunkt Technik: „Die Dachkonstruktion ruht auf zehn Modulen, die sich wie ihre Kollegen im Natatorium elegant nach unten verjüngen, und auch sie werden wiederum durch polygonale Glasflächen getrennt. Sie sind an den Enden der Kragarme verbunden, wobei immer zwei Module geometrisch identisch ausgebildet und, bezogen auf die Mittelachse des Gebäudes, symmetrisch angeordnet wurden." (*Deutsche BauZeitschrift*, 11/2011) Die Länge der Träger und die Höhe variieren, und auf diese Weise entsteht der fast runde Grundriss, der jeweils seitlich angeschnitten wurde.

Die halbmondförmige Tribüne des Freiluftstadions der Weltmeisterschaften (dem dritten „Kiesel") und nunmehrigen Freibades variiert das Thema der übergangslosen Dachwand ein weiteres Mal. Die Outdoorarena benötigt keine durchgehende Außenwand und der „Skelettaufbau" ist offener, wirkt leichter als bei den anderen beiden Bauten. Das vom Rand her auskragende Dach läuft in die sichelförmig aufgestellten trapezförmigen Stützelemente über. Es entsteht ein einfaches in sich stabiles „Raum"-Tragwerk. Es beschützt die Sprunganlage und das 50-m-Becken. Von dort aus haben Zuschauer einen freien Blick auf den Fluss Huangpu und die Turmspringer können das Gefühl haben, in die aufregende Stadtlandschaft Shanghais zu fliegen.

Zu nah dran?

› Wir haben über Wahrnehmung gesprochen. Über das Fernsehen und den Stadtmaßstab. Trotz ihrer Größe behalten die Baukörper eine unerwartete Leichtigkeit. Die Längsseiten der Multifunktionshalle wirken in der Ansicht zum Wasser und bei abendlicher Lichtinszenierung wie ein großes gläsernes Tor. Und auch sonst haben die Architekten hier und am Natatorium ihre geometrischen Großformen, den Wechsel von Wand und Öffnung, leicht gemacht. Die „Skulptur" zeigt gleichzeitig Haut und Knochen, es wurde nicht monolithisch, sondern in

Good architecture is not just about images and allegories, comparisons and symbols, but about architectural, urban and landscape spaces. It is in particular the last mentioned that we find at the SOSC, because the interiors are devoted above all to their respective functions, or need to be flexible like a film studio in their use, interchangeable.

Outside, the composition of the open spaces initially follows a Chinese approach, so to speak. The three stadium buildings are harnessed to artificial lakes, creating a kind of macro feng shui feeling. The entrances to the sports campus are oriented to the south. (In China, the enemy always came from the north, as did and does the cold wind from Mongolia.) The ancient Chinese theme, namely the motif of a nature-religion water park landscape, is played out here. gmp architects have now overlaid this green and blue sports campus with three hall complexes: Beginning with the so-called Natatorium containing several daylit swimming pools over a length of 220 meters. It occupies a privileged position by the main square with the underground rail station. This is only logical because the Natatorium has become a public swimming pool in its subsequent life. During the World Championships the pools were used mainly for training. The Natatorium spans the boundary between campus and city. However, the outside edge of the swimming hall does not come across as a rigid border; the roof trusses, which are cladded in double-curved aluminum panels and spill over the façade, are interrupted by triangular glass surfaces. This opening and closing of the façades creates the impression of arcades. Due to the repeated rhythm between truss and opening, these arcades appear light and loose, despite the length of the building.

5

This is followed in the "hinterland" by a multi-purpose arena which was used as the main competition venue for swimming during the FINA World Championships. It holds 18,000 spectators. During my visit, the icing equipment was being installed under the hall floor. The arena is now a hybrid space for sports, concerts, and other cultural events. No swimming takes place here anymore, but it has not become a white elephant either. The hall with a diameter of 130 to 140 meters and clear height of forty-five meters and positioned on a six-meter-high reinforced concrete plinth, has a main façade and roof construction made of parallel triangular trusses on an almost circular ground plan. At that time, I wrote the following in a review focusing on the technical aspects:

"The roof construction rests on ten modules which, like their fellows in the Natatorium, taper down elegantly, and they too are in turn separated by polygonal glass surfaces. They are connected at the ends of the cantilevers, with two modules that are always being geometrically identical and, in relation to the central axis, arranged symmetrically." (*Deutsche BauZeitschrift*, 11/2011) The length of the girders and the height vary, resulting in the almost circular ground plan, which is indented at each side.

The crescent-shaped stands of the outdoor stadium of the World Championships (the third so-called pebble) and now open-air pool are another variation on the theme of the transition-free roof-wall. The outdoor arena does not require a continuous outer wall, and the skeleton structure is more open and appears lighter than the other two buildings. The overhanging edge of the roof flows into the crescent-shaped, trapezoidal support

Schichten gedacht. Die Tragwerksstruktur[5] beinhaltet Dreigurte und wird mit zweiseitig gekrümmten Aluminiumpaneelen verkleidet. Das gilt für das Outdoorstadion und die Indoorstadien, für die rechteckigen und runden Grundrisse.

Das konstruktiv aufwändige Projekt ist in Zusammenarbeit mit den Ingenieuren von schlaich bergermann und partner entstanden, das heißt das architektonische Konzept bekam sehr früh eine grundsätzliche Trag-Idee zugeordnet: Die Grundstruktur des Natatoriums ist ein schlanker Bogen mit geringem Stich; zwei leicht gespreizte Fachwerkebenen verstärken ihn. Daraus entwickelt sich der Baukörper. 13 dieser Bögen mit variierender Spannweite (86 bis 95 Meter) reihen sich im Abstand von 17 Metern entlang der Hauptachse und werden durch eine Sekundär- bzw. Pfettenstruktur untereinander verbunden. Sie bilden gemeinsam mit dazwischen gehängten Oberlichtern die Dachkonstruktion der Schwimmhalle. Der gläsern umschlossene Hallenkörper steht innerhalb der gereihten Formen. Bei der großen Multifunktionsarena wird dieses Prinzip auf einen runden und hohen Raum übertragen und ein Zweigelenkrahmensystem gewählt, das Halle und Foyer gleichzeitig einbezieht. Die Spannweite der zehn einzelnen Rahmen ist mit 80 bis 150 Metern recht unterschiedlich.

Solch komplexes Denken kann inzwischen umgesetzt werden, weil wir entsprechend digital agieren und parametrisch konstruieren können - wobei der Kritiker an dieser Stelle anmerken muss: Der Architekt denkt sich die Geometrie zwar aus, aber ohne den Ingenieur wäre sie in dieser Tragweite nicht rechenbar. Allen drei Sportstätten ist gemeinsam, dass die Tragformen auf im Grundriss geschwungene Linien aufgesetzt sind und sie in sich bzw. an ihren Kanten aus geschwungenen, meist kreisförmigen Linien bestehen. Die innere Tragstruktur und äußere Hülloberfläche werden hier, müssen hier zusammen gedacht werden. Die Achse Architekt-Ingenieur hat hier vorbildlich funktioniert und konnte zum Leistungsträger für Eleganz und Leichtigkeit werden. In einem anderen Punkt haben die Architekten einlenken müssen. Geplant war ein „keramischer" Charakter, der an chinesische Porzellanarbeiten erinnert und das Leichte im Schweren unterstützt hätte. Glasfaserverstärkter Beton, der solche Effekte hätte vermitteln können, wurde von chinesischer Seite aus technischen Erwägungen und vergabepolitischen Gründen nicht akzeptiert, stattdessen wurden doppelt gekrümmte Aluminiumpaneele mit weiß beschichteter Oberfläche eingesetzt - vielleicht die übliche, aber insgesamt in der Nahsicht trotzdem eine befriedigende Lösung. „Es ist gelungen, eine Stadionfamilie zu generieren, deren Dächer die Funktion des Tragverhaltens bildlich überhöhen - aus Freude an der kräftigen Konstruktion", schrieb ich damals in der *Deutschen BauZeitschrift* unter dem direkten Einfluss des erlebten Besuches. Ich denke, diese Aussage hat weiterhin Bestand. Architekten nennen das auch expressiv. Ein bisschen erinnert das an das Schönheitsideal von muskulösen Schwimmern. Architekten und Kritiker leben zwar in anderen Welten, aber es sind vor allem Sportler, die hier zu Hause sein sollen.

Verantwortlich für diese Wahrnehmungen mag das China-Syndrom des immer Schnelleren und Größeren sein. Wir in Deutschland verstehen das nicht so richtig, können es nur schwer deuten, weil man solche Aufgaben gar nicht mehr in der Heimat bauen darf oder kann. Und wenn, dann sowieso kleiner, transparenter und spielerischer. Olympia in München war 1972. Deutsche Architekten und Ingenieure, die in China arbeiten, geraten zu Hause schnell in eine eigentlich absurde Rechtfertigungshaltung. Der Kritiker gleich mit. Denn die Besonderheiten der Aufgabe - Maßstab und Schnelligkeit am Bau - und der daraus resultierende architektonische Ausdruck werden unterschätzt oder oft falsch fokussiert. Es hilft, näher dran zu sein und lokal im globalen Dorf zu sein. Hingucken und Anfassen hilft - jedes Haus ist auch zu globalen Zeiten immer noch lokal verortet. Eine gute Beurteilung hat mit Perspektive, Nähe und Zeit zu tun. Hier war sie möglich.

elements, resulting in a simple, intrinsically stable spatial supporting structure. It protects the diving area and the fifty-meter pool. From here the spectators have a clear view of the Huangpu River, and the divers have the sense of flying into the exciting cityscape of Shanghai.

Too close?

› We spoke about perception. About television and city scale. In spite of their size, the buildings retain an unexpected lightness. Seen from the water and in the evening light, the sides of the main arena look like a large glass gate. Here and on the Natatorium, the architects have also lent a lightness to their large geometrical forms, the alternation of wall and opening. The sculpture-like structure shows skin and bones at the same time; they were not thinking monolithically, but in layers. The supporting structure contains triangles and is cladded with double-sided curved aluminum panels. This applies to the outdoor and indoor stadia, and to the rectangular and round floor-plans.

The structurally complex project was created in cooperation with the engineers schlaich bergermann und partner, which means that, from a very early stage, a fundamental conception of the support framework underlay the overall architectural approach: the basic structure of the Natatorium is a slim arch with a slight rise, reinforced by two slightly splayed truss levels. It is from this that the structural shell emerges. Thirteen of these arches with varying spans (eighty-six to ninety-five meters) stand at intervals of seventeen meters along the main axis and are connected to each other by a secondary or purlin structure. Together with the skylights suspended between them, they form the roof construction of the Natatorium. The glass-encircled hall shell stands inside the rows. In the large multi-purpose arena this principle is transferred to a round, high space and a double-jointed frame, which incorporates the hall and the foyer at the same time. The spans of the ten individual frames vary considerably between 80 and 150 meters.

In the meantime, such complex thinking can be put into practice because we can act digitally and design parametrically, though the critic must note at this point: the architect may be the one to come up with the geometry, but without the engineer it would not be calculable on this scale. What all three sports venues have in common is that the supporting forms are placed on curved lines in the ground plan and that they consist of curved, mostly circular lines in themselves and at their edges. The inner supporting structure and outer shell surface are and must be considered together. The architect-engineer axis functioned in an exemplary fashion here, becoming the driving force for elegance and lightness.

At another point the architects were compelled to intervene. A ceramic-like character was planned, which is evocative of Chinese porcelain and would have supported the idea of lightness within heaviness. Glass fiber reinforced concrete, which could have conveyed such effects, was not accepted on the Chinese side due to technical considerations and procurement policy reasons. Double-curved aluminum panels with a white coated surface were used instead—perhaps an orthodox solution but overall a satisfactory one, nevertheless, especially when seen at close quarters. "A stadium family has been generated whose roofs figuratively elevate the function of the load-bearing properties—as if expressing joy at the powerful construction," I wrote in the *Deutsche BauZeitschrift*, inspired by my visit there. I think that this statement still holds. Architects also call it expressive. It is slightly reminiscent of the aesthetics of muscular swimmers. Architects and critics may live in different worlds, but it is above all athletes who are meant to be at home here.

The China syndrome of faster and bigger may be responsible for these perceptions. In Germany, we do not really understand it, and we find it hard to interpret because we may and can no longer build such projects in this country. And if we do, then it takes place on a smaller, more transparent and more playful scale. The Olympic Games in Munich—that was in 1972. German architects and engineers working in China quickly find themselves in the frankly absurd position of having to justify themselves in their home country. As do the critics. The peculiarities of the task—scale and speed in construction—and the resulting architectural expression are underestimated or frequently misunderstood. It helps to be closer and to be local in the global village. Looking and touching helps—each house is also localized in global time. A good appraisal has to do with perspective, proximity, and time. Here it was possible.

Fotografische Dokumentation/ Pläne und Zeichnungen

Photographic Documentation/ Plans and Drawings

S20
济阳路
Jiyang Rd
耀华路 上南路
出口

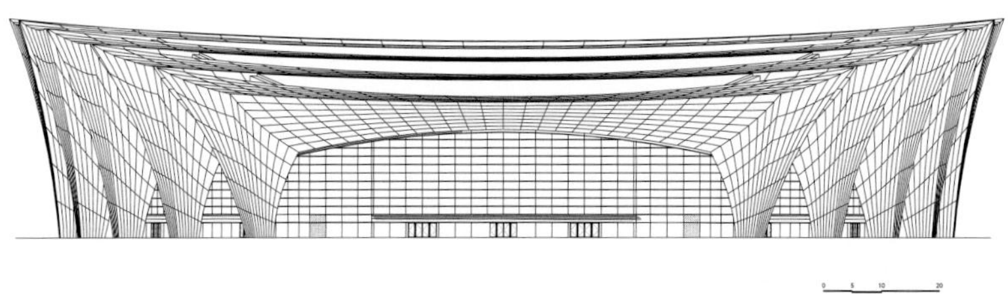

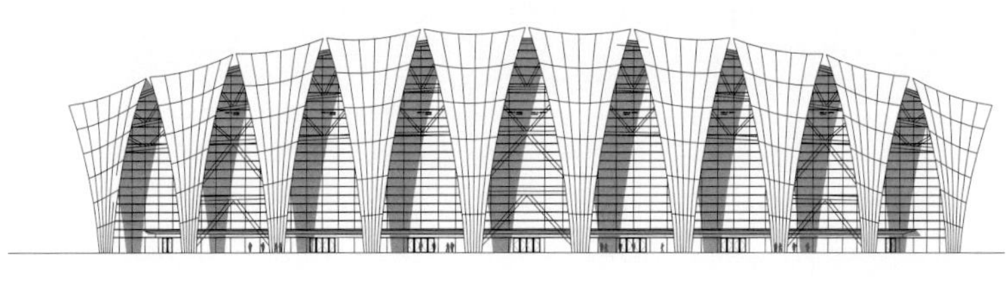

↑ Ost-/Westansicht mit konkaver Dachkrümmung
East/west elevation with concave roof curvature

↑ Nord-/Südansicht mit konvexer Dachkrümmung
North/south elevation with convex roof curvature

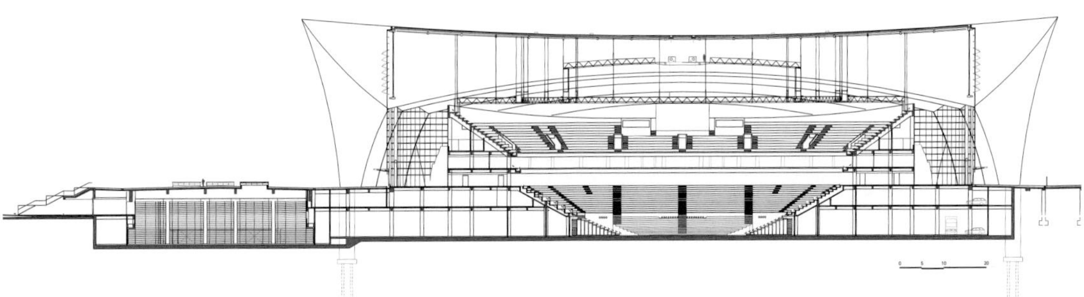

Längsschnitt
Longitudinal section

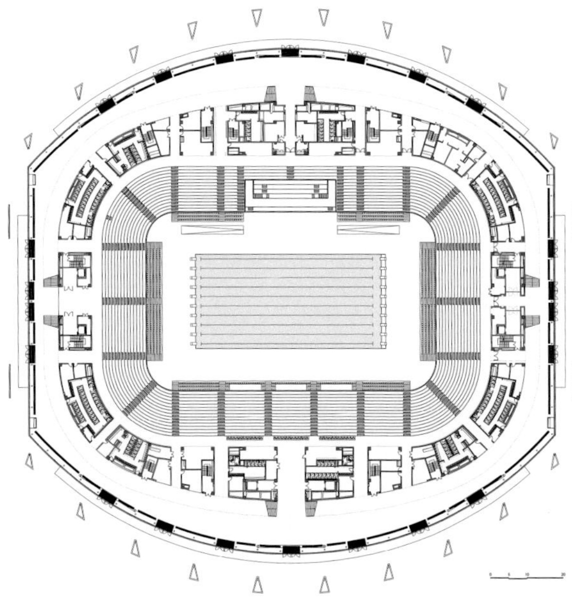

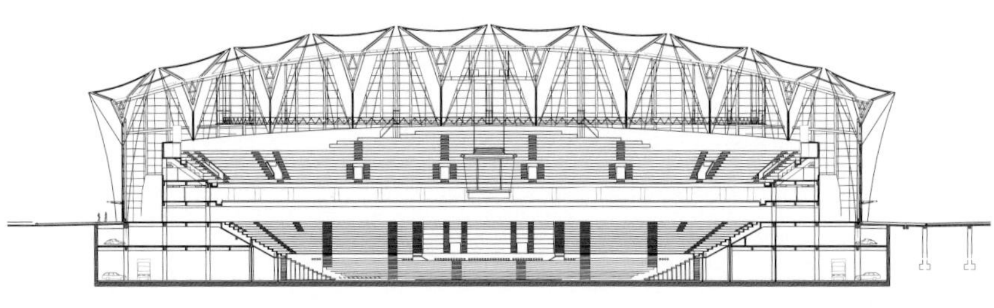

Grundriss Eingangsebene
Floor-plan entrance level

↑ Querschnitt
Cross section

↗ Grundriss mittlere Ebene/VIP-Bereich
Floor-plan central level/VIP area

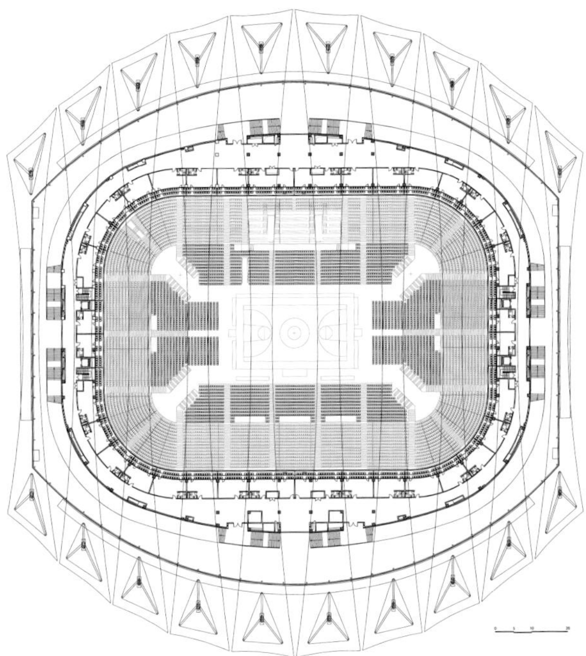

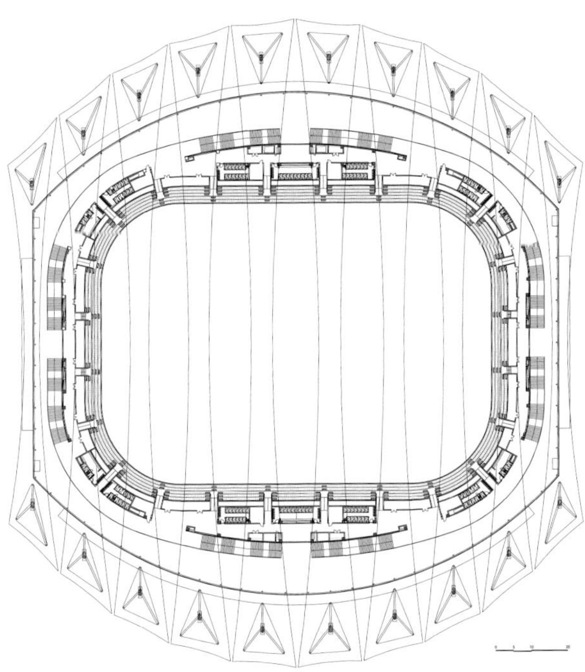

↑ Grundriss obere Ränge
Floor-plan upper tiers

7

Die Hauptkonstruktion des geschlossenen Hallenstadions mit runder Grundrissfläche besteht aus Stahlbeton, das Dach aus einer 170 Meter überspannenden Stahlkonstruktion mit Aluminiumverkleidung.
The main structure of the closed multi-purpose stadium with a round plan consists of reinforced concrete, while the roof is a steel structure with a 170-meter span with aluminum cladding.

Fassadendetail
Detail of façade

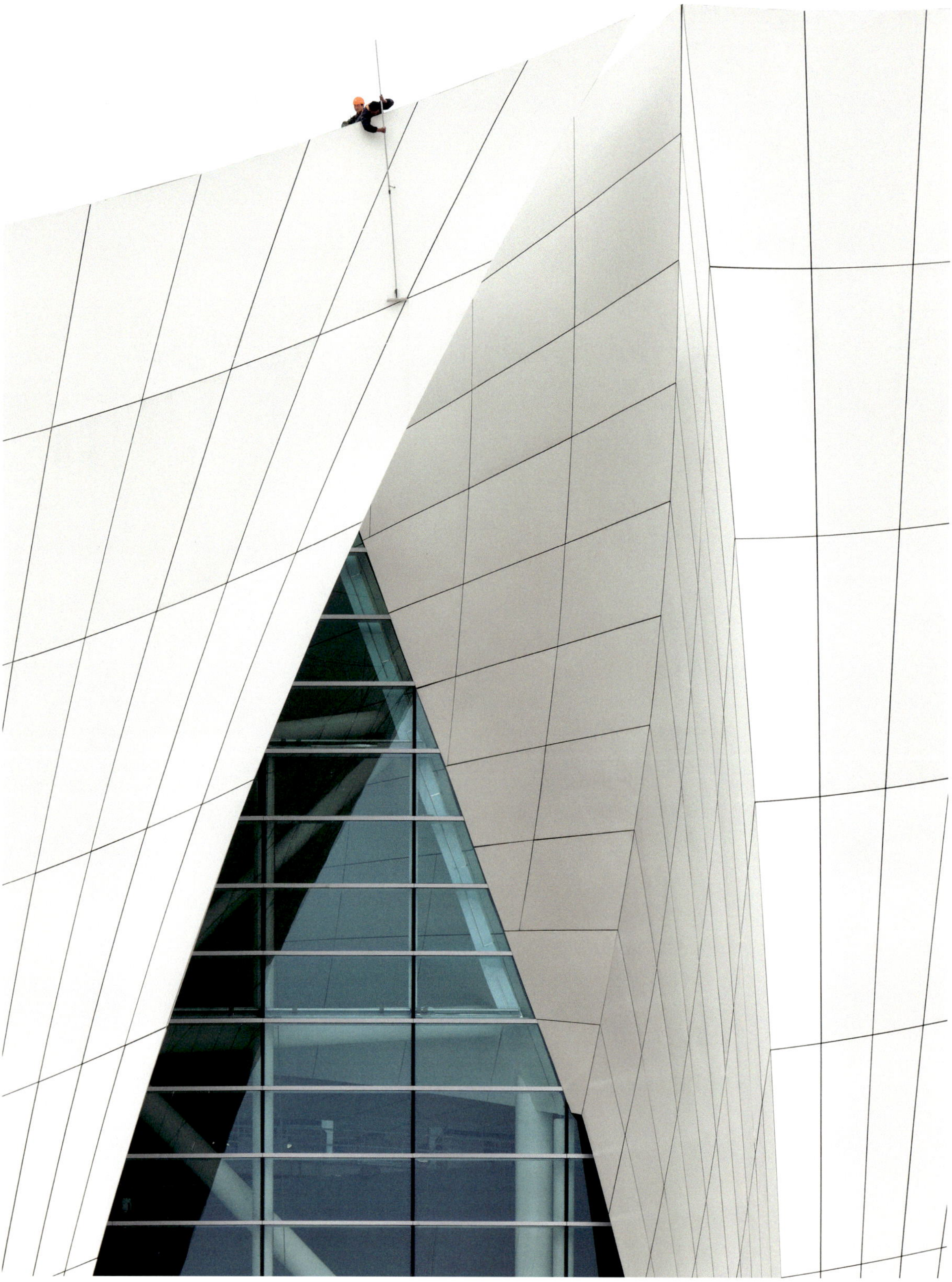

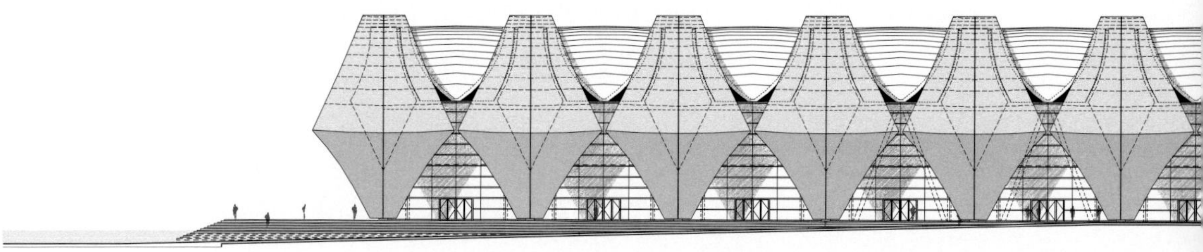

Ansicht Süd
South elevation

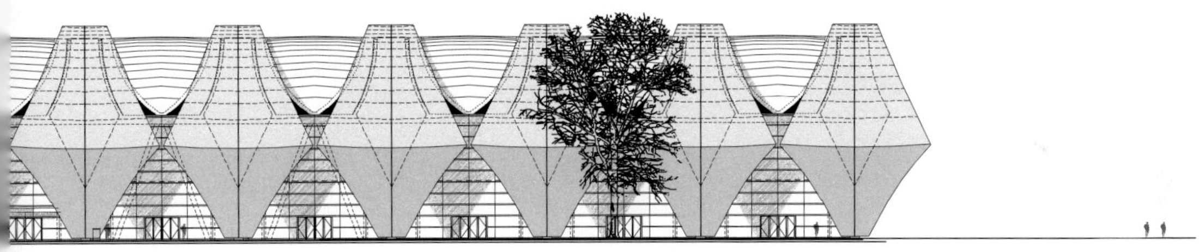

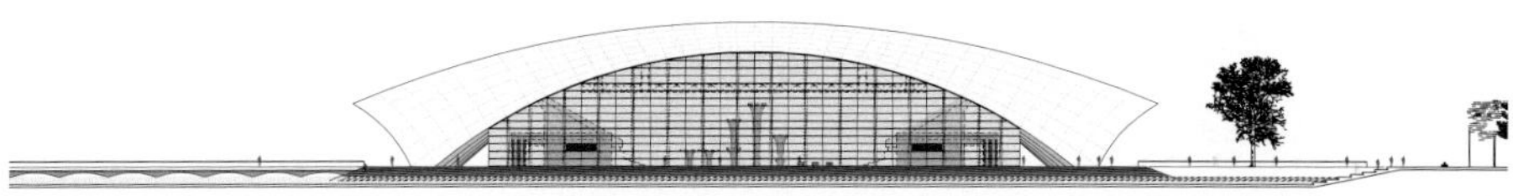

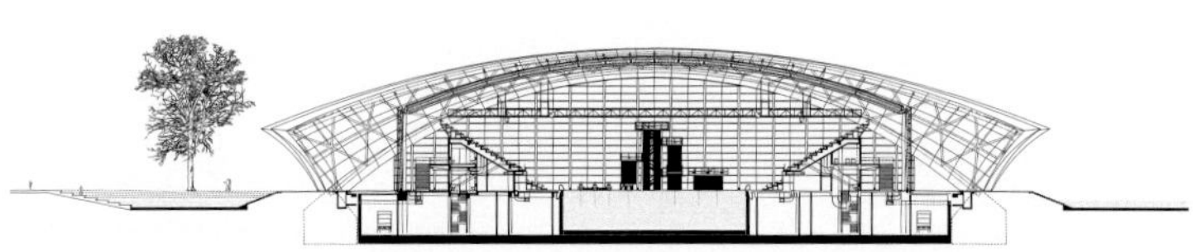

↑ Ansicht vom Fluss Huangpu
Elevation from the Huangpu River

↑ Querschnitt Sprungbecken
Cross section diving pool

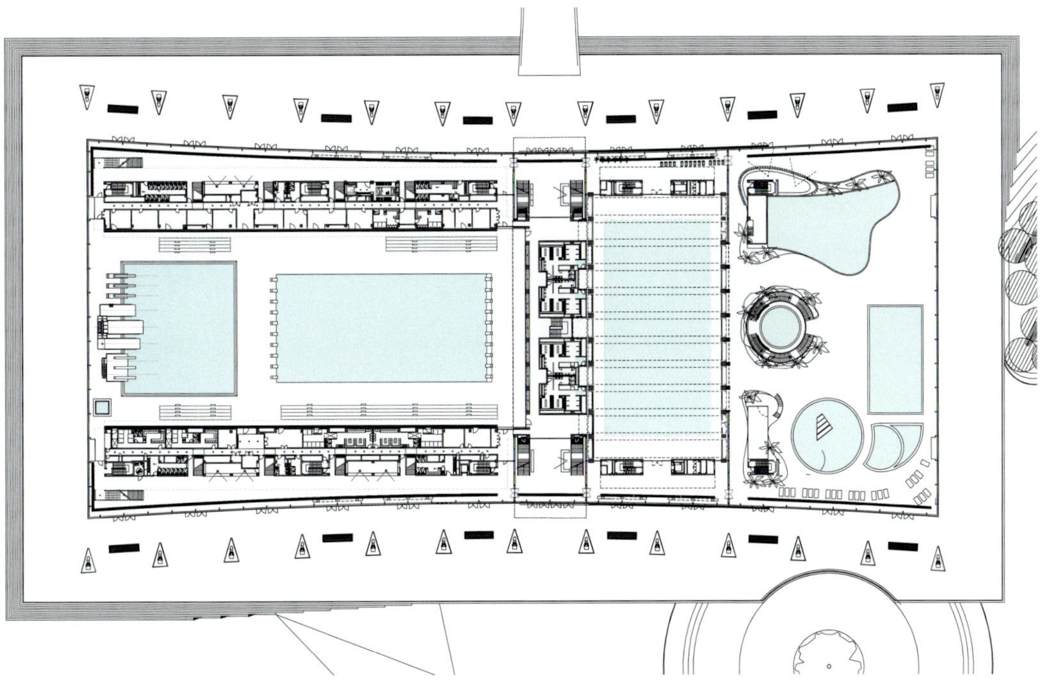

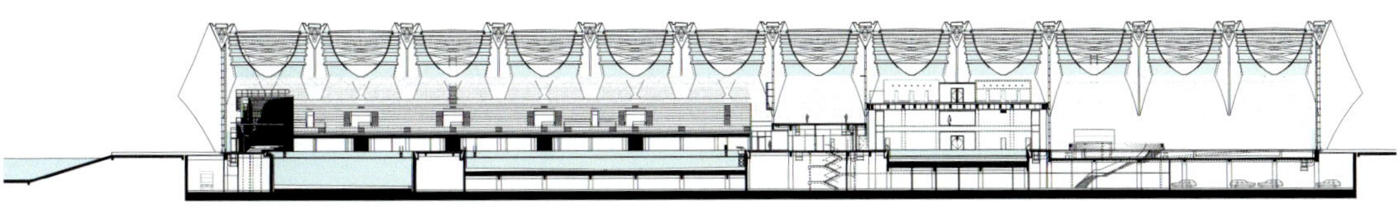

↑ Grundriss
Floor-plan

↑ Längsschnitt
Longitudinal section

Die Stahlkonstruktionen aus weitgespannten Bögen mit großformatigen Dreiecks-elementen aus beschichteten Aluminiumblechen bilden entlang der Rahmen der Unterkonstruktionen zweiseitig gekrümmte Flächen und zitieren damit Segel im Wind.
The steel structures of broad arches with large-format triangular elements made of coated aluminum sheet form double-sided curved surfaces along the frame of the sub-structures, thus evoking sails in the wind.

Die Strukturelemente selbst sind sichtbar, die Konstruktionselemente verkleidet.
The structural elements themselves are visible, but the construction elements are cladded.

→→ ◫ Das Innere des Natatoriums
Inside the Natatorium

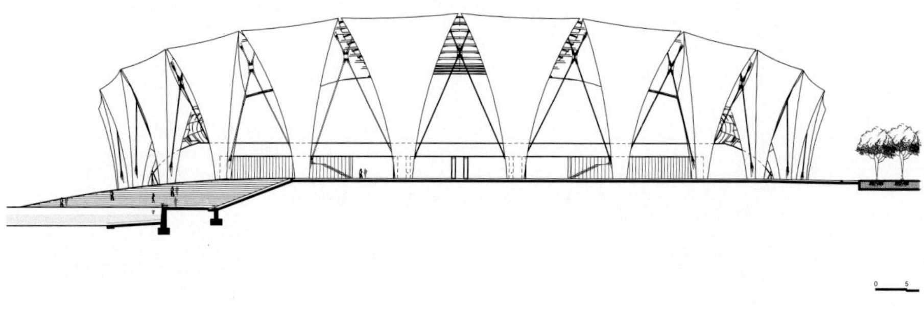

Ansicht Ost
East elevation

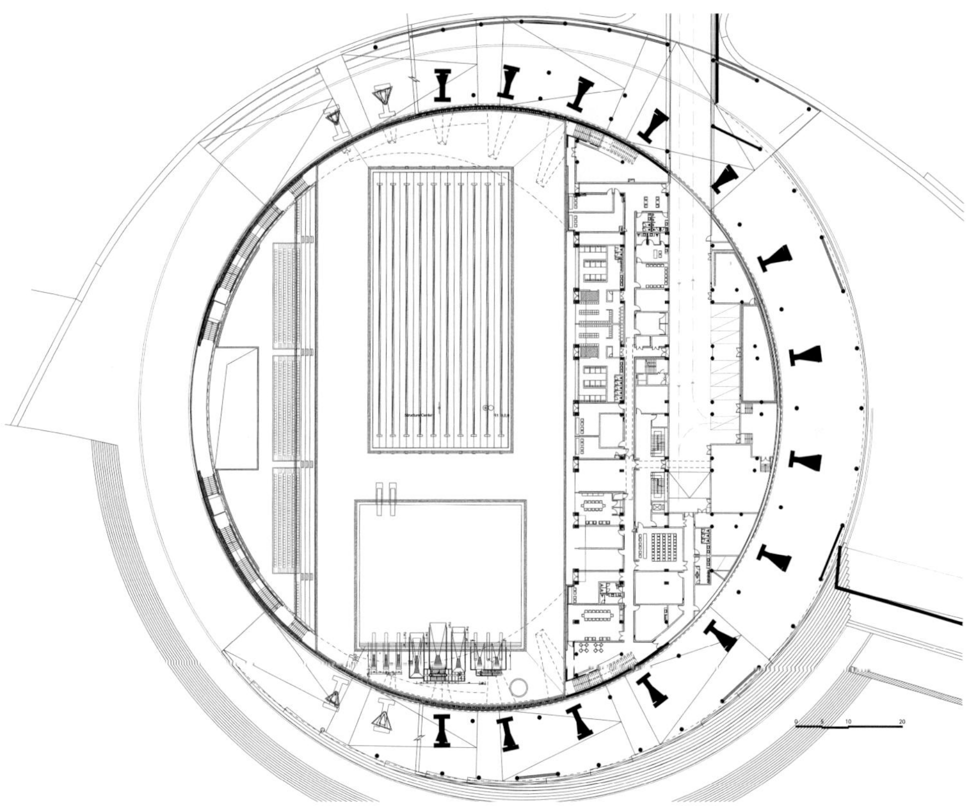

Grundriss Ebene 0 (Schwimmbecken und Umkleiden)
Floor-plan level 0 (swimming pool and changing rooms)

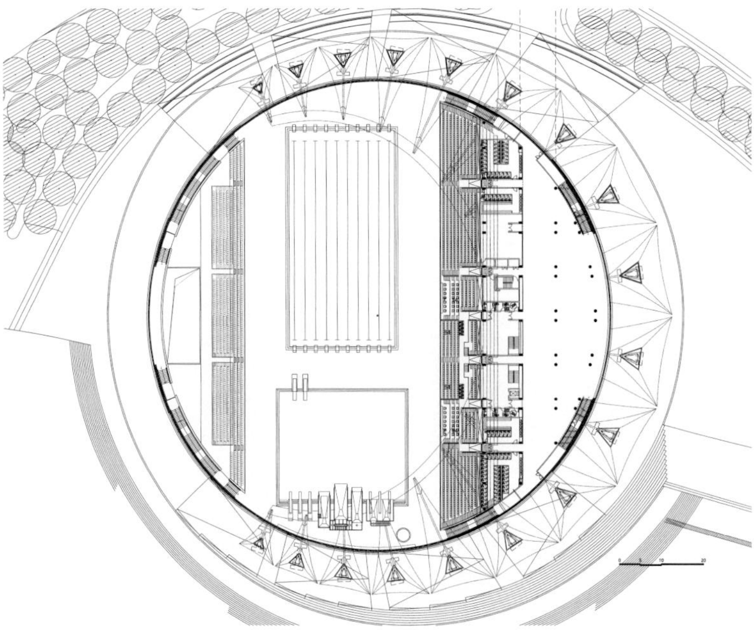

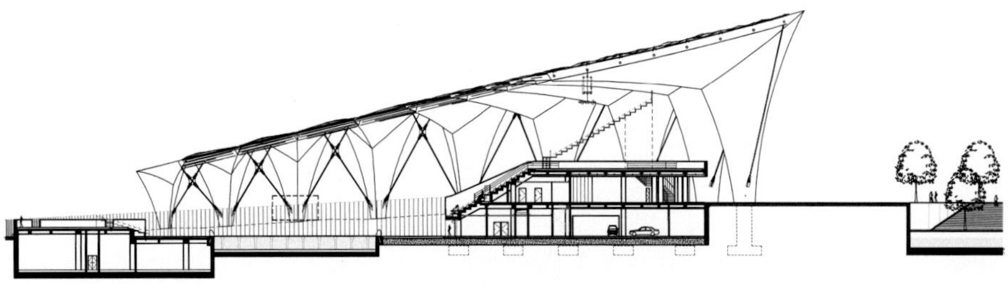

↑ Grundriss Ebene 1 (Zuschauerbereich)
Floor-plan level 1 (spectator area)

↑ Schnitt
Section

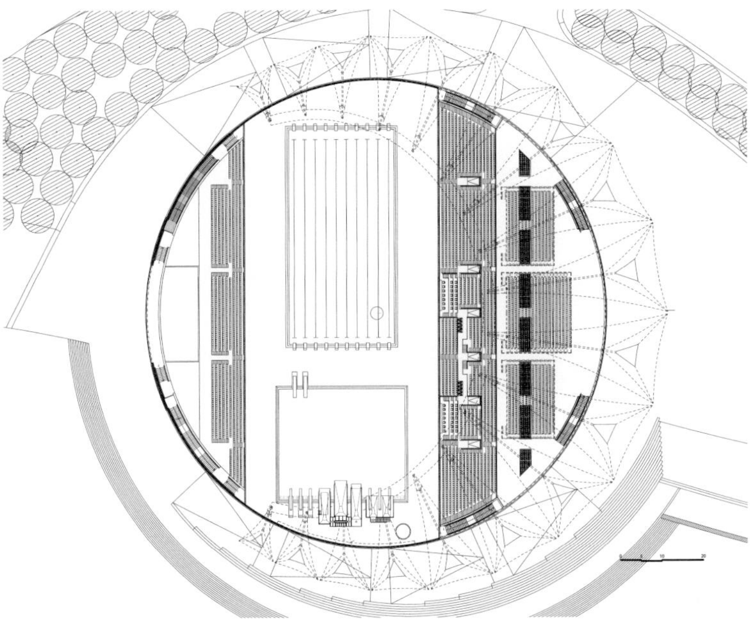

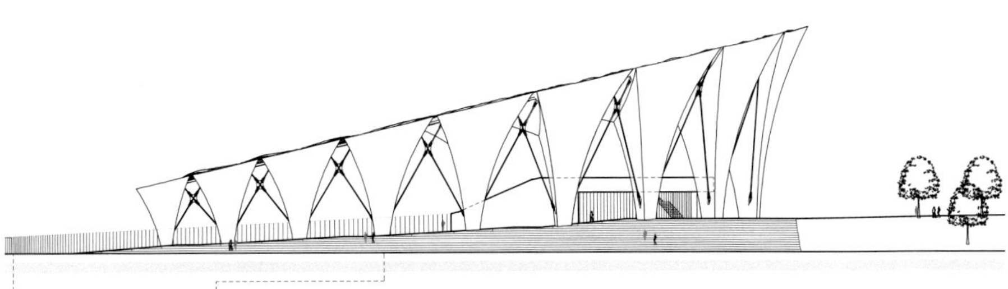

↑ Grundriss Ebene 2 (Zuschauerränge)
Floor-plan level 2 (tiers)

↑ Ansicht Süd
South elevation

◫ ← Mit einem äußeren Durchmesser von ca. 130 Metern spiegelt die Dachkonstruktion des Außenschwimmbeckens den runden Grundriss der Gebäudehülle wider.
The roof structure of the outdoor swimming pool with its external diameter of approx. 130 meter reflects the round ground-plan of the shell of the building.

↑ Im Außenschwimmstadion mit Sprungturmanlage wird die halbrunde Tribünenüberdachung durch radial angeordnete Kragarme mit dazwischen gespannten leichten Membranen gebildet.
In the outdoor swimming stadium with its diving platform, the semi-circular arena roof consists of radially arranged cantilevers with lightweight membranes spanned between them.

Außenschwimmstadion und Medienzentrum
Outdoor swimming stadium and media center

Anhang

Appendix

gmp Entwurfsteam Design Team

Meinhard von Gerkan

Prof. Dr. h. c. mult. Dipl.-Ing. Architekt BDA

geboren 1935 in Riga (Lettland). Gemeinsam mit Volkwin Marg gründete von Gerkan 1965 gmp Architekten von Gerkan, Marg und Partner. Schon am Beginn seiner Karriere stand mit dem Flughafen Tegel ein bedeutendes Projekt, dem zahlreiche weitere bis heute folgten. 1974 wurde von Gerkan von der Universität Braunschweig auf den Lehrstuhl für Entwerfen berufen, 2005 erhielt er die Ehrendoktorwürde durch die Chung Yuan Christian University in Chung Li (Taiwan). Das East China Normal University College of Design in Shanghai verlieh von Gerkan 2007 eine Ehrenprofessur, 2014 ernannte ihn die Tongji University zum Advising Professor. Von Gerkan ist Mitglied der Freien Akademie der Künste zu Hamburg und hat zahlreiche weitere Auszeichnungen erhalten, unter anderem den Fritz-Schumacher-Preis, den Rumänischen Staatspreis, den Großen Preis des Bundes Deutscher Architekten und das Bundesverdienstkreuz.

Born in 1935 in Riga, Latvia, von Gerkan founded gmp Architekten von Gerkan, Marg and Partners with Volkwin Marg in 1965. The beginning of his career was marked by an important project–Tegel Airport–which has been followed by many others to this day, including the main railway station in Berlin and the planning of the 1.3-million city of Lingang. In 1974 von Gerkan was appointed to the Chair for Design by Braunschweig University, and in 2005 he was awarded an honorary doctorate by Chung Yuan Christian University in Chung Li, Taiwan. The East China Normal University College of Design in Shanghai awarded von Gerkan an honorary professorship in 2007, and Tongji University in Shanghai appointed him Advising Professor in 2014. He set up the gmp Foundation and the Academy for Architectural Culture for the advancement of gifted young architects. Von Gerkan is a member of the Freie Akademie der Künste, Hamburg and has received numerous other awards such as the Fritz Schumacher prize, the Romanian State prize, the Association of German Architects Grand Award and the Federal Cross of Merit.

Nikolaus Goetze

Dipl.-Ing. Architekt

geboren 1958 in Krefeld. 1987 schloss er sein Studium an der RWTH Aachen mit dem Diplom ab. Ein DAAD-Stipendium führte ihn 1985 in die Meisterklasse von Prof. W. Holzbauer, Hochschule für angewandte Künste, Wien. Seit mehr als 25 Jahren ist er als Architekt im Büro von Gerkan, Marg und Partner tätig, seit 1998 als Partner. Nikolaus Goetze ist unter anderem verantwortlich für die Großprojekte Grand Theatre Chongqing, Masterplanung und Maritim-Museum für Lingang New City, Shanghai, Hanoi Museum und Nationalparlament in Hanoi. Aktuelle Arbeitsschwerpunkte in Deutschland sind unter anderem der Neubau für die Kunsthalle Mannheim und das Designzentrum für Audi in Ingolstadt. Als Mitinitiator der aac - Academy for Architectural Culture - ist er maßgeblich an der Veranstaltung von Workshops beteiligt. Verschiedene Workshops standen bisher unter seiner Leitung.

Born in 1958 in Krefeld, Goetze graduated from RWTH Aachen University, completing his diploma in 1987. A DAAD grant enabled him to attend the master class of Prof. W. Holzbauer at the University of Applied Arts in Vienna in 1985. He has been working as an architect for von Gerkan, Marg and Partners for more than twenty-five years and, in 1998, became a partner. Nikolaus Goetze is responsible for the following large projects, among others: Grand Theatre Chongqing, the masterplan and Maritime Museum for Lingang New City, Shanghai, the Hanoi Museum, and the National Parliament in Hanoi. Several current key projects in Germany are the new construction of the Kunsthalle Mannheim and the Design Centre for Audi in Ingolstadt. As co-initiator of the aac–the Academy for Architectural Culture–he plays a significant role in workshops organized by the aac. To date he has led a number of workshops.

Magdalene Weiss

Dipl.-Ing. Architekt

geboren 1964 in Bopfingen. Weiss studierte Architektur in Stuttgart und Kassel und kam 1997 zu gmp, wo sie seit 2010 assoziierte Partnerin ist. Weiss ist vorwiegend in China tätig und hat dort verschiedene Projekte betreut, unter anderem das COMAC Headquarter in Shanghai, das Shanghai Oriental Sports Center, die SOHO Beijing Residence oder das Poly Plaza in Shanghai. In Deutschland war sie beteiligt am Swissôtel Berlin am Kurfürstendamm.

Born in 1964 in Bopfingen, Weiss studied architecture in Stuttgart and Kassel and joined gmp in 1997, where she has been an associated partner since 2010. Weiss works primarily in China and has completed a number of projects there, such as the COMAC headquarters in Shanghai, the Shanghai Oriental Sports Center, the SOHO Beijing Residence and the Poly Plaza in Shanghai. In Germany, she was involved with the Swissôtel project in Berlin at Kurfürstendamm.

Chen Ying

M. Arch.

geboren 1969 in Shanghai (China). Chen studierte Architektur an der Tongji Universität in Shanghai und arbeitete danach für das East China Architectural Design Institute. 2006 kam sie zu gmp, wo sie 2011 Direktorin im Büro in Shanghai wurde. Chen hat in Shanghai zahlreiche Projekte betreut, darunter das Caohejing Pujiang Metro Plaza und das Shanghai Oriental Sports Center.

Born in 1969 in Shanghai, China, Chen studied architecture at Tongji University in Shanghai and then worked for the East China Architectural Design Institute. In 2006 she joined gmp, where she is a director at the Shanghai office. Chen has been responsible for numerous projects in Shanghai, including the Caohejing Pujiang Metro Plaza and the Shanghai Oriental Sports Center.

gmp Partner China

Wu Wei

Dipl. Architekt ETH

geboren 1971 in Lanzhou/Gansu (China). Wu studierte Architektur in Chongqing, China und war von 1992 bis 1994 als Architekt in Lanzhou und Shanghai tätig, ehe er von 1994 bis 1995 in der Schweiz Deutsch studierte. An der ETH Zürich nahm er ein weiteres Architekturstudium auf, das er 2000 mit dem Diplom bei Prof. Mario Campi abschloss. Nach Tätigkeiten für Skyline Architecture und bei Swiss-German Consulting in Zürich kam Wu 2000 zu gmp, wo er zunächst Chefrepräsentant der Büros in Peking und Shanghai war, 2004 assoziierter Partner wurde und 2009 Partner für China.

Born in 1971 in Lanzhou, Gansu, China, Wu studied architecture in Chongqing in China and, from 1992 to 1994, practiced architecture in Lanzhou and Shanghai before he studied German in Switzerland between 1994 and 1995. He then undertook further architectural studies at the ETH Zurich, which he completed in 2000 with a diploma under Professor Mario Campi. After working for Skyline Architecture and SwissGerman Consulting in Zurich, Wu joined gmp in 2000 where he started as chief representative of the Beijing and Shanghai offices and then became an associate partner in 2004 and partner for China in 2009.

Autoren und Fotografen Authors and Photographers

Dirk Meyhöfer
Autor und Journalist Author and Journalist

geboren 1950 in Herne/Westfalen. Studium der Architektur in Hannover. Nach dem Diplom zehn Jahre Redakteur im Jahreszeitenverlag in Hamburg, hauptsächlich für *Architektur und Wohnen*.
Seit 1987 ist Meyhöfer freiberuflicher Architekturjournalist und -publizist und schreibt unter anderem für *Süddeutsche Zeitung*, *Der Spiegel*, *KUZ online*, *WDR*, *DLF*, *DBZ*. Er hat über 60 Bücher zu Stadt und Architektur veröffentlicht und zahlreiche Ausstellungen kuratiert. Seit 1989 ist er Herausgeber des Jahrbuchs *Architektur in Hamburg*. Meyhöfer lehrt unter anderem an der HCU Hamburg und der Detmolder Schule für Architektur und Innenarchitektur.

Born in 1950 in Herne, Westphalia, Meyhöfer studied architecture in Hanover. Following his graduation, he was editor at the Jahreszeiten publishing house in Hamburg for ten years, mostly working for *Architektur und Wohnen* magazine. Since 1987, Meyhöfer has worked as a freelance architectural journalist and author, writing for *Süddeutsche Zeitung*, *Der Spiegel*, *KUZ online*, *Westdeutscher Rundfunk*, *Deutschlandfunk*, *Deutsche Bauzeitung*, among others. He has published over sixty books on cities and architecture and has been the curator of numerous exhibitions. Since 1989, he has been publishing the *Architektur in Hamburg* yearbook. Meyhöfer holds teaching assignments at HafenCity University Hamburg and the Detmold School of Architecture and Interior Design.

Marcus Bredt
Fotograf Photographer

geboren 1968 in Göttingen. Am Lette-Verein in Berlin wurde Bredt von 1992 bis 1994 zum Fotografen ausgebildet. Er spezialisierte sich früh auf Architekturfotografie und hat für internationale Auftraggeber gearbeitet, etwa für Daniel Libeskind oder Sauerbruch Hutton. gmp begleitet Bredt seit 2004 weltweit mit seinen Aufnahmen. Er hat nationale Projekte wie den Berliner Hauptbahnhof ebenso dokumentiert wie internationale zum Beispiel in China, Vietnam, Südafrika und Brasilien. Bredt lebt in Berlin.

Born in 1968 in Göttingen, Bredt trained as a photographer at the Lette Association in Berlin between 1992 and 1994. He specialized in architectural photography from early on and has worked for international clients such as Daniel Libeskind and Sauerbruch Hutton. Bredt has been taking photographs for gmp all over the world since 2004. He has documented national projects, such as Berlin's main railway station, as well as international ones, for example, in China, Vietnam, South Africa, and Brazil. Bredt lives in Berlin.

Projektdaten Project Data

Bauherr Client
Shanghai Administration of Sports

Intern. Wettbewerb Int'l. competition
2008 – 1. Preis 1st prize

Entwurf Design
Meinhard von Gerkan und and Nikolaus Goetze
mit with Magdalene Weiss

Projektleitung Project Management
Chen Ying

Mitarbeiter Entwurf (alphabetisch) Design Staff (in alphab. order)
Jan Blasko, Rebekka Brauer, Fang Hua, Fu Chen, Martin Hagel, Lü Cha, Lü Miao, Alexander Schober, Song Mo, Sun Gaoyang, Nina Svensson

Mitarbeiter Ausführung Planning Staff
Jan Blasko, Fang Hua, Martin Friedrich, Fu Chen, Sun Gaoyang, Ilse Gull, Jin Zhan, Kong Rui, Lin Yi, Katrin Löser, Lü Cha, Lü Miao, Jörn Ortmann, Ren Yunping, Alexander Schober, Nina Svensson, Tian Jinghai, Yan Lüji, Zhang Yan, Zhou Yunkai, Zhu Honghao

Statik Structural Engineering
schlaich bergermann und partner, Sven Plieninger

Landschaftsplanung Landscaping
WES & Partner, Michael Kaschke

Chinesische Partnerbüros Chinese Partner Practices
SIADR, Tongji Design Institute

Haustechnikplanung Technical Equipment
ARUP

Bauzeit Construction Period
2009–2011

BGF insgesamt GFA in total
157 000 m²

Kapazitäten Capacity

Hallenstadion Multi-purpose Stadium
18 000 Sitzplätze seats

Natatorium
5 000 Sitzplätze seats

Außenschwimmstadion
Outdoor Swimming Pool
5 000 Sitzplätze seats

Bildnachweis Picture Credits

Marcus Bredt
Titelmotiv Cover
Bildstrecke Spreads
Seiten Pages 6–7, 32–33, 38–47, 52–63, 68–87

gmp
Seiten Pages 16, 34–37, 48–51, 64–67
gmp/Magdalene Weiss
Seite Page 17

Frontop
Seiten Pages 18–19, 21

Heiner Leiska
Seite Page 23

ullsteinbild
Seite Page 22
1 Reuters/Yorgos Karahalis
Seite Page 24
2 Euroluftbild.de/Frank Herzog
Seite Page 25

Jan Siefke
Seite Page 27

ON Grafik – Hamburg
1 modifizierte Welt- und Chinakarte
modified World and China map
http://d-maps.com
2 Karte Shanghai-Stadtgebiet
Map of Shanghai–City area
http://www.openstreetmap.org
Seiten Pages 8–9, 11

Danksagung Acknowledgement

Besonderer Dank gilt dem Projektteam für die Begleitung der Publikation, insbesondere Fanny Hoffmann-Loss.
Special thanks to the project team for supervising the publication, particularly to Fanny Hoffmann-Loss.

Impressum Imprint

Konzept Concept
Michael Kuhn gmp
Leiter PR und Kommunikation Head of PR

Herausgeber Editors
Meinhard von Gerkan gmp
Nikolaus Goetze gmp

Koordination Editorial Direction
Carolina López gmp
Xiaoshi Fang gmp

Layoutkonzept und Satz Layout and Typesetting
ON Grafik, Tom Wibberenz mit with
Hendrik Sichler, Hamburg

Korrektorat Proofreading
Anja Bippus (dt.)
Mara Taylor (engl.)

Übersetzung Translation
Ian McCaughtrie
Hartwin Busch (Lebensläufe curricula vitae)

Bildredaktion und -bearbeitung Picture Editing
Trixi Hansen gmp
Guido Brixner gmp

Reproduktion Reproduction
DZA Druckerei zu Altenburg GmbH

Druck und Bindung Print Production and Binding
DZA Druckerei zu Altenburg GmbH

Papier Paper
Multi Art Silk von by Papyrus Europe
150 g/m²

Schrift Font
Linotype Avenir Next Pro

Titelmotiv Cover Picture Christian Gahl
Bibliografische Information der Deutschen Nationalbibliothek
Bibliographic information published by the Deutsche Nationalbibliothek
Die Deutsche Nationalbibliothek verzeichnet diese Publikation in der Deutschen Nationalbibliografie; detaillierte bibliografische Daten sind im Internet über http://dnb.d-nb.de abrufbar.
The Deutsche Nationalbibliothek lists this publication in the Deutsche Nationalbibliografie; detailed bibliographic data are available on the internet at http://dnb.d-nb.de

jovis Verlag GmbH
Kurfürstenstraße 15/16
10785 Berlin

www.jovis.de

ISBN 978-3-86859-333-4